THE WORLD OF PLANTS

WHAT DO ROOTS, STEMS, LEAVES, AND FLOWERS DO?

by Ruth Owen

PowerKiDS
press.

New York

Published in 2015 by The Rosen Publishing Group, Inc.
29 East 21st Street, New York, NY 10010

First Edition

Produced for Rosen by Ruby Tuesday Books Ltd
Editor for Ruby Tuesday Books Ltd: Mark J. Sachner
US Editor: Joshua Shadowens
Designer: Emma Randall

Photo Credits:
Cover, 4–5, 6–7, 9, 10 (right), 11, 12, 14, 16, 17 (top), 18–19, 20–21, 22–23, 24, 25 (bottom), 26–27 © Shutterstock; 8, 28–29 © Ruby Tuesday Books; 10 (left) © Superstock; 13 © Istockphoto; 15 © FLPA; 17 (bottom) © Science Photo Library; 25 (top), 25 (center) © Wikipedia Public Domain.

Library of Congress Cataloging-in-Publication Data

Owen, Ruth, 1967–
 What do roots, stems, leaves, and flowers do? / by Ruth Owen. — First edition.
   pages cm. — (The world of plants)
 Includes index.
 ISBN 978-1-4777-7137-2 (library binding) — ISBN 978-1-4777-7138-9 (pbk.) —
 ISBN 978-1-4777-7139-6 (6-pack)
 1. Plants—Juvenile literature. 2. Roots (Botany)—Juvenile literature. 3. Stems (Botany)—Juvenile literature. 4. Leaves—Juvenile literature. 5. Flowers—Juvenile literature. I. Title. II. Series: World of plants (New York, N.Y.)
 QK49.O97 2015
 580—dc23

2014007550

Manufactured in the United States of America

CPSIA Compliance Information: Batch #WS14PK8: For Further Information contact Rosen Publishing, New York, New York at 1-800-237-9932

Contents

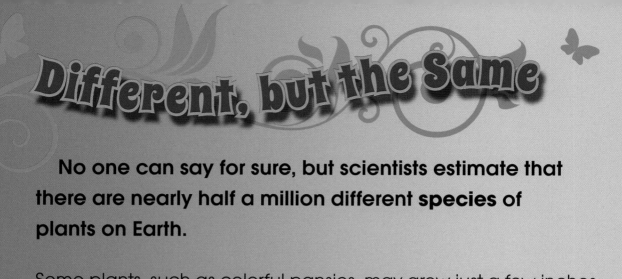

No one can say for sure, but scientists estimate that there are nearly half a million different **species** of plants on Earth.

Some plants, such as colorful pansies, may grow just a few inches (cm) high. Giant redwood trees, however, can grow higher than a 25-story building!

Giant redwood trees

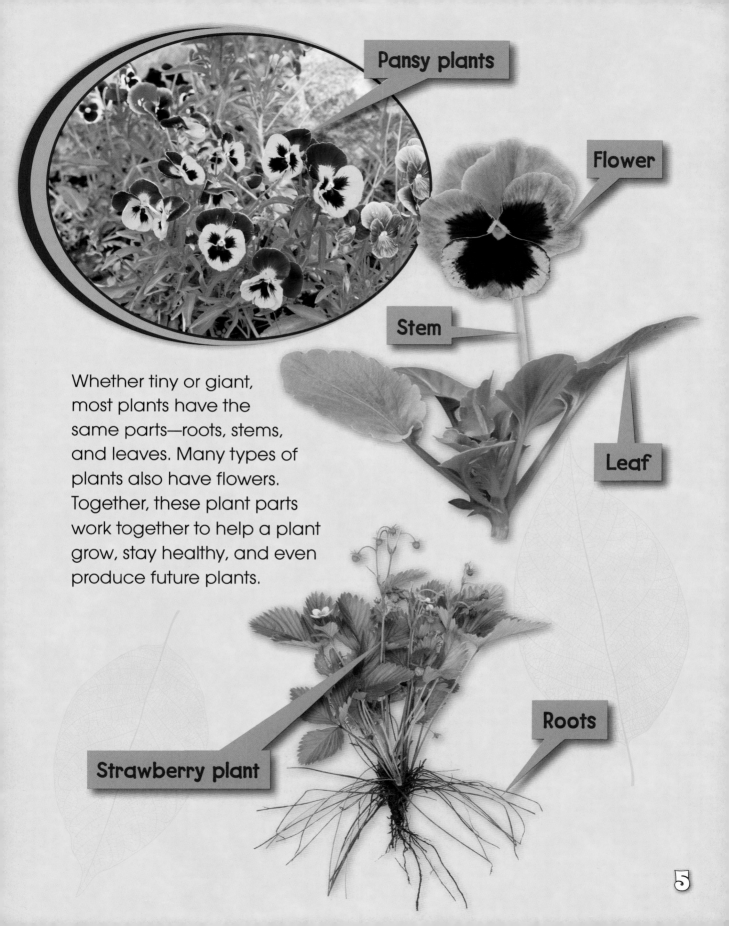

Pansy plants

Flower

Stem

Leaf

Whether tiny or giant, most plants have the same parts—roots, stems, and leaves. Many types of plants also have flowers. Together, these plant parts work together to help a plant grow, stay healthy, and even produce future plants.

Strawberry plant

Roots

Roots for Food and Water

The roots of most plants are hidden underground in soil.

Some plants have many roots that spread out in the soil horizontally. Trees usually have this type of root. A large tree may have woody roots as thick as a person's arm. Thinner, hair-like roots grow from the thick roots.

Other plants have one main root that grows down into the ground. This long, thick root is called a **taproot**. Dandelions and carrot plants have taproots. The orange carrots we eat are actually the thick taproots of carrot plants.

Trunk

Roots

Carrot plant

Taproot

In order to be healthy, plants need water and **nutrients**, such as nitrogen, potassium, and calcium. A plant's roots act like drinking straws, taking in water and nutrients, which are dissolved in water, from the soil.

Roots for Stability

Roots do more than supply a plant with water and nutrients. They also hold a plant in the soil and give it stability.

Without roots, most plants would topple over when the wind blows or as their branches, leaves, or flowers grow and became heavy. The roots of a large tree may spread underground in an area two or three times the diameter of the tree's branches. Many trees survive for years on steep slopes because their roots hold the trees steady in the soil.

Tree branches and leaves

Spread of tree roots underground

This tree lives on a steep slope and has been blown sideways by the wind. Its roots still hold it in place!

A dandelion is also a good example of how roots can anchor a plant in soil. Try tugging one of these little plants out of the ground, and you will likely end up with only a handful of leaves and stems. The dandelion's taproot will stay firmly underground!

Dandelion plant

Taproot

A Plant's Stems

A plant's stems support the plant, acting like a framework.

Thinner stems grow from a plant's main stem and connect to its leaves or flowers. On a tree, stems that grow from the plant's main stem (or trunk) are known as branches. The branches connect to even thinner stems, called twigs, where the leaves grow.

A plant's stems contain a system of tubes called **xylem** and **phloem**. The xylem tubes carry water and nutrients from the roots through the plant's stems to its leaves. A plant's leaves act like little food factories making food for the plant. The phloem tubes carry this food from the leaves to wherever it is needed inside the plant.

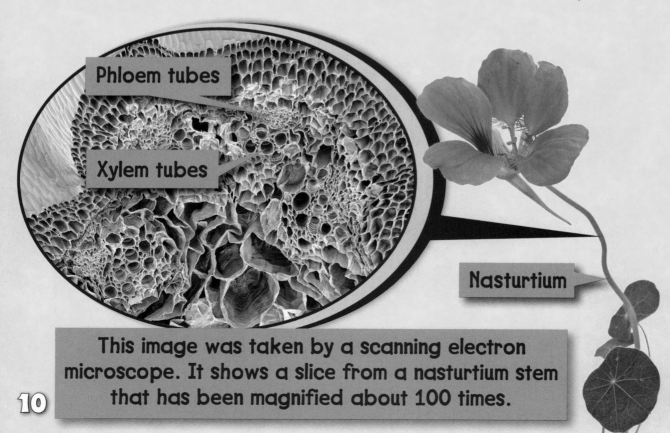

Phloem tubes

Xylem tubes

Nasturtium

This image was taken by a scanning electron microscope. It shows a slice from a nasturtium stem that has been magnified about 100 times.

Record-Breaking Stems

In the world of plants, stems are often the plant part responsible for breaking records.

A giant redwood tree in Redwood National Park in California is currently the tallest tree on Earth. The record-breaking tree, named Hyperion, has grown to 379 feet (116 m) tall. That's over 70 feet (21 m) taller than the Statue of Liberty! It's possible, however, that one day an even taller tree might be discovered.

The 2,000-year-old Tule tree in Santa María del Tule, Mexico, has one of the thickest trunks on Earth. At its widest point, the tree's trunk measures 114 feet (35 m) across. That's wider than the length of a basketball court.

The Tule tree

Bamboo is a type of thick-stemmed grass plant from Asia. The stems of one species of giant bamboo can grow up to three feet (1 m) in a single day!

Giant bamboo is a fast-growing huge species of grass.

Leafy Food Factories

From long and thin, to small and rounded, spiky, shiny, huge, and tiny—leaves come in many shapes and sizes.

The leaves of some plants are smaller than a dime. Others are enormous, like the gunnera, or giant rhubarb, plant's leaves, which can grow to over 10 feet (3 m) across.

All leaves have a very important job to do—they make food for the plant. A plant may take in nutrients from the soil, but that's like you taking vitamins. To grow and remain healthy, you also need proper meals to give you energy. A plant is the same. It needs a type of sugary food for energy. It makes this food using water, **carbon dioxide** from the air, and sunlight.

A gunnera, or giant rhubarb, plant

Leaves for Photosynthesis

When a plant makes food in its leaves using sunlight, water, and carbon dioxide, the process is called photosynthesis.

Photosynthesis takes place with the help of a substance called **chlorophyll**. It's the chlorophyll in plants that gives them their green color.

The chlorophyll in a plant's leaves traps the energy in sunlight. Water is delivered to the leaves from the roots. The leaves take in carbon dioxide from the air through **microscopic** holes called **stomata**. Once the ingredients are in place, a plant's leaves use sunlight to turn the water and carbon dioxide into a sugary plant food.

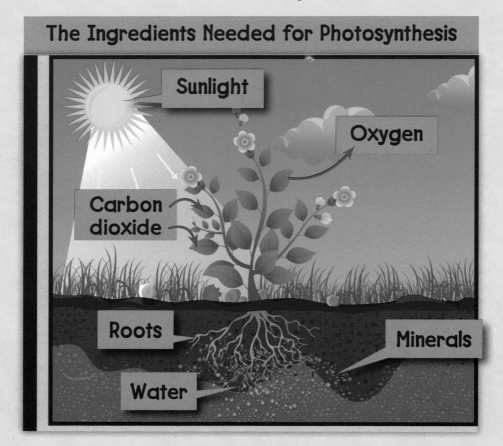

The Ingredients Needed for Photosynthesis

Sunlight

Oxygen

Carbon dioxide

Roots

Minerals

Water

Stomata on a potato plant leaf, as seen under a microscope

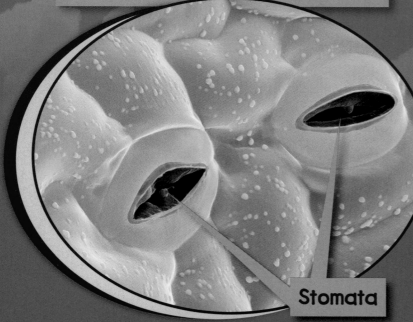

Stomata

During photosynthesis, something else important happens. Plants make oxygen and release it from the stomata in their leaves. Without plants, humans and other animals would have no oxygen to breathe!

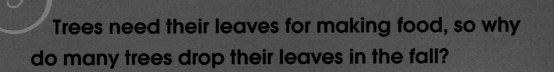

Fall Leaves

Trees need their leaves for making food, so why do many trees drop their leaves in the fall?

During winter, the days are short, with few hours of sunlight. There is often less rain in winter, too, and water in the soil may freeze. With little sunlight and water available, a tree's leaves cannot make enough food to feed the tree. Growing and keeping leaves healthy uses a lot of energy, too. So, in readiness for the tough winter months, many trees drop their leaves in the fall. The tree then stops growing and rests until spring to save energy.

In the fall, many tree leaves turn brown, red, or yellow. This is because when the leaves stop making food, they also stop making green chlorophyll. This allows the leaves' other colors, which are normally hidden by green, to show through.

Evergreen Leaves

The leaves of many types of coniferous, or evergreen, trees look like thin, green needles.

Just like on other plants, however, each needle is able to use sunlight, water, and carbon dioxide to make food for the tree.

Coniferous trees often live in tough **habitats** where sunlight and water are in short supply all year round. So these trees don't drop all their leaves in fall. Instead, they lose and regrow small quantities of leaves all year long. Having leaves all year allows coniferous trees to make food whenever they get the chance. Also, growing a whole new set of leaves each spring uses up a lot of energy. So coniferous trees keep their leaves and save their energy!

Needles

Each thin pine needle shown here is a leaf.

Coniferous trees growing in a tough, cold habitat

21

Flowers for Reproduction

Many plants, including trees, grow flowers. These plant parts enable flowering plants to **reproduce** by making seeds.

Stigma

Style

Anther

Colorful petals attract insects to the flower.

Filament

Stem

Seeds form deep inside the flower.

Leaf

Flowers produce a dust called **pollen** on their anthers. The pollen from one flower, a lily for example, must be carried to the stigma of another lily. The lily with pollen on its stigma is now **pollinated** and is ready to begin making seeds.

Some flowers are pollinated by the wind blowing their pollen from flower to flower. Other flowers need help from animals such as insects, birds, and bats. When an animal, such as a butterfly, lands on a flower, some pollen sticks to its body. Then the butterfly flies off and visits a different flower of the same kind. Some of the pollen on the butterfly's body brushes off and sticks to that flower's **stigma**.

A butterfly pollinating a lily flower

Making Seeds

After a plant's flowers have been pollinated, seeds begin to form inside the flowers.

Seeds grow inside plant parts that protect them as they grow. A poppy plant's seeds, for example, form inside a hard, hollow case called a seedpod. The seeds of an apple tree grow inside protective fruits that we know as apples. In time, the plant's flowers die leaving only the fruit or seedpod behind.

Poppy flower

A seedpod forming

Fully-formed poppy seedpods

1

2

3

Poppy seeds

Split seedpod

Once the seeds are fully grown, a seedpod will split open. The seeds fall to the ground, where they can grow into new plants. Apples and other fruits fall to the ground, too. Then the fruits rot away, allowing the seeds inside to settle on the soil, ready for growing.

1 Apple blossom flower

2 Dying flower

An apple forming

3 Protective fruit

Seeds

A New Plant

Once a seed is settled in some soil, it usually waits for spring before starting to grow.

First, roots grow from the seed into the soil. Next a seedling, or shoot, grows from the seed. Then tiny leaves sprout from the seedling. The seedling's roots and stems deliver water to the leaves. The young leaves take in carbon dioxide and use sunlight to begin making food for the plant. The new plant grows bigger and stronger. In time, if it's a flowering plant, it will grow flowers for making seeds.

Leaf

Stem

A runner bean seedling

Roots

Seed

A runner bean plant may take just weeks to grow. A tree may take hundreds of years. However long its life, the different parts of a plant keep working together to help the plant grow, stay healthy, and reproduce.

A runner bean plant with flowers

People eat the seedpods of runner bean plants.

You will need:
- Water
- A glass
- A teaspoon
- Blue food coloring
- A knife and cutting board
- A celery stalk with leaves

INVESTIGATION 1: Stems in Action

A plant's stems contain tubes that deliver water from the roots to the rest of the plant. See this in action in this investigation.

Step 1:
Put 1 inch (2.5 cm) of water into the glass.

Step 2:
Mix two teaspoons of blue food coloring into the water.

Step 3:
Using a knife, carefully cut 1 inch (2.5 cm) from the bottom of the celery stalk.
(Only use a knife if an adult is there to help you.)

Step 4:
Stand the celery stalk in the blue water. Over the next few days, the celery stalk and leaves will turn a blue or bluish color.

Day 1

Day 3

Why? How? What?

Why do you think the celery stalk and leaves have turned blue?

(See page 32 for the answer.)

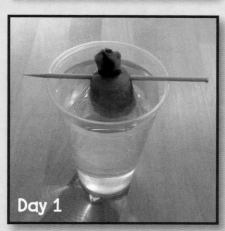

You will need:

- A small glass
- Water
- A carrot
- A knife and cutting board
- A wooden skewer

Day 1

Day 10

INVESTIGATION 2: Roots in Action

A tasty, crunchy orange carrot is actually the main taproot of a carrot plant. You can't grow a new carrot for eating from a piece of taproot, but you can grow a new carrot plant!

Step 1:
Fill the glass with water to about 0.5 inch (1.25 cm) from the top.

Step 2:
Cut about 1 inch (2.5 cm) from the top of the carrot. **(Only use a knife if an adult is there to help you.)**

Step 3:
Push the skewer through the carrot top and then balance the skewer on the top of the glass so the carrot is touching the water.

Step 4:
Put the glass in a sunny place. Top off and refresh the water in the glass every few days.

Step 5:
Within a few days, you'll see stems and leaves growing from the top of the piece of carrot root. Tiny threadlike roots may even begin sprouting from the piece of carrot.

Day 10

Why? How? What?
How is the piece of carrot helping the new leaves to grow?
(See page 32 for the answer.)

29

Glossary

carbon dioxide
(KAHR-bun dy-OK-syd)
A clear gas in the air that plants use to make food. When humans and other animals breathe out, they release carbon dioxide into the air.

chlorophyll (KLOR-uh-fil)
The substance that gives plants their green color. Leaves use chlorophyll for making food during photosynthesis.

coniferous (kah-NIH-fur-us)
Referring to trees that often grow in cold, tough habitats and do not lose their leaves in winter. Many have needlelike leaves.

habitats (HA-buh-tats)
Places where animals or plants normally live. A habitat may be a backyard, a forest, the ocean, or a mountainside.

microscopic (my-kreh-SKAH-pik)
So small that an object can only be seen through a microscope and not with just a person's eyes alone.

nutrients (NOO-tree-ents)
Substances needed by a plant or animal to help it live and grow. Plants take in nutrients from the soil using their roots. The nutrients in soil are dissolved in water.

phloem (FLOH-em)
Tubes inside a plant that carry food from the leaves through the stems to wherever it is needed inside the plant.

photosynthesis
(foh-toh-SIN-thuh-sus)
The process by which plants make food in their leaves using water, carbon dioxide, and sunlight.

pollen (PAH-lin)
A colored dust made on the anthers of flowers, which plants need in order to reproduce.

pollinated (PAH-luh-nayt-ed)
When pollen is carried from the anthers of one flower to the stigma of another. Some flowers need pollen from another flower of the same species in order to be

pollinated. Other types of flowers are able to self-pollinate. This means pollen from the flower's anthers can be transferred to its own stigma.

reproduce (ree-pruh-DOOS)
To make more of something, such as when plants make seeds that will grow into new plants.

species (SPEE-sheez)
One type of living thing. The members of a species look alike and can reproduce together.

stability (stuh-BIH-luh-tee)
The ability to be stable, which in the case of a plant means standing upright and not falling over.

stomata (STOH-muh-tuh)
Microscopic holes on a leaf that a plant uses for taking in carbon dioxide and releasing oxygen.

taproot (TAP-root)
A thick main root of a plant that grows down into the soil. Often, some thin, hair-like roots grow from a taproot.

xylem (ZI-lum)
Tubes inside a plant that carry water from the roots, through the stems, and to the leaves.

Websites

Due to the changing nature of Internet links, PowerKids Press has developed an online list of websites related to the subject of this book. This site is updated regularly. Please use this link to access the list:

www.powerkidslinks.com/wop/roots/

Read More

Aitken, Stephen. *Plants and Insects*. New York: Cavendish Square Publishing, 2014.

Appleby, Alex. *What Happens in Fall?* New York: Gareth Stevens, 2014.

Edwards, Nicola. *Leaves*. New York: PowerKids Press, 2008.

Index

Answers

INVESTIGATION 1:
The xylem tubes in the celery stalks have carried the blue water through the stalks and up to the leaves, dyeing them blue.

INVESTIGATION 2:
The piece of carrot taproot is taking in water just as the root would if it was in soil. Having water and sunlight allows the carrot plant to start growing new leaves.